BIBLIOGRAPHY

T &

Francisco Coronado

and the Exploration
of the American Southwest

Explorers of New Worlds

Francisco Coronado
and the Exploration
of the American Southwest

Hal Marcovitz

Chelsea House Publishers
Philadelphia

Prepared for Chelsea House Publishers by:
OTTN Publishing, Warminster, PA

CHELSEA HOUSE PUBLISHERS
Editor in Chief: Stephen Reginald
Managing Editor: James D. Gallagher
Production Manager: Pamela Loos
Art Director: Sara Davis
Director of Photography: Judy L. Hasday
Senior Production Editor: LeeAnne Gelletly
Series Designer: Keith Trego

3 5 7 9 8 6 4 2

Library of Congress Cataloging-in-Publication Data

Marcovitz, Hal.
    Francisco Coronado / by Hal Marcovitz.
    p.   cm. – (Explorers of new worlds)
    Summary: A biography of the conquistador whose quest
for the Seven Cities of Gold led to the exploration of the
American Southwest in 1540.
    ISBN 0-7910-5515-9 (hc)
    1. Coronado, Francisco Vásquez de, 1510-1554 Juvenile
literature. 2. Southwest, New–Discovery and exploration–Spanish Juvenile literature. 3. Southwest, New–
Gold discoveries Spanish Juvenile literature. 4. Indians of
North America–First contact with Europeans–Southwest,
New Juvenile literature. 5. Explorers–America Biography Juvenile literature. 6. Explorers–Spain Biography
Juvenile literature. [1. Coronado, Francisco Vásquez de,
1510-1554. 2. Explorers. 3. America–Discovery and
exploration.] I. Title. II. Series.
E125.V3M34   1999
917.904'1–dc21
                                                    99-35228
                                                          CIP

Contents

The Seven
Cities
of Gold

Spanish military leader Francisco Vásquez de Coronado and his men marched through the dusty deserts of the Southwest hunting for the elusive Seven Cities of Gold.

I

The army had trekked for a thousand miles over the most unforgiving terrain on earth: broad and barren deserts, populated mostly by scorpions, cactus, and sagebrush, and steep mountains, where the dusty trails were barely wide enough for the men to lead their horses in single file. The soldiers were forced to cross rivers with swift, rushing currents, and to make their way through dried lava beds, where the ash left over from long-forgotten, prehistoric volcanoes would blacken their shoes. At night, they shivered around their campfires. During the day, the scorching temperatures climbed well over 100 degrees. The men on the expedition would call the area **despoblado**—a Spanish word meaning "uninhabited area" or, more precisely, "desolate wilderness."

The soldiers were Spanish. They were members of an army led by 29-year-old Francisco Vásquez de Coronado. He had been placed in command of the army by the **viceroy** of the Spanish colony of New Spain. The colony included the lands of modern-day Mexico and had as its capital Mexico City.

The mission of Coronado and his men was to find the Seven Cities of Gold. They believed that each city would bring them riches. They were going on the word of **Fray** Marcos de Niza, a religious brother and mapmaker who had traveled north from Mexico in 1539, returning with magnificent stories of the Seven Cities. (Fray, pronounced "fry," is a Spanish title meaning "friar.")

"The cities were surrounded with walls, with their gates guarded, and were very wealthy, having silversmiths; and the women wore strings of gold beads and the men girdles of gold and white woolen dresses; and they had sheep and partridges and slaughterhouses and iron forges," Fray Marcos told one of his servants.

The men dreamed of taking some of the gold for themselves. The viceroy of Mexico wanted the gold, and so did the king of Spain. The king was very interested in the *expedition*, and he gave the mission his blessing.

The army had left Compostela, a city several hundred miles northwest of Mexico City, on the morning of February 23, 1540. They headed north. Three hundred soldiers— 240 *cavalry* soldiers and 60 foot soldiers—had signed up for the journey. They were armed with crossbows and *arquebuses*, long guns that shot tiny lead balls. The arquebus had to be reloaded with ball and gunpowder after each shot. Neverthe-less, in its day it was an effective weapon. It was much deadlier than the spears and bows carried by the hostile Indians the soldiers expected to meet.

> **Coronado was so confident he would succeed that he spent some 50,000 *ducats* of his own money on the expedition—an incredible sum in the 16th century. Today, that money would be worth well over $1 million.**

Also, each soldier wore heavy armor breastplate and helmet. Coronado's armor was **gilded**, or plated with gold. It was shined to a hard gloss. Adorning his helmet was a large, colorful feather.

In addition to the soldiers, 800 Indians armed with spears, bows, and huge wooden swords edged with flint went on the expedition. Hundreds more Indians were brought along as servants. Black slaves from Africa had been forced to go along as well. They were expected to do camp chores and tend to the more than 1,000 pack animals and the several hundred cattle, sheep, and pigs making the journey as a traveling food supply.

"It was the most brilliant company ever assembled to go in search of new lands," wrote Pedro de Castaneda, a foot soldier on the expedition, who would go on to chronicle Coronado's travels for the next two and a half years.

It was not an easy journey. The men were not accustomed to the rough terrain and the harsh elements. Some were injured or became ill and died.

"We found no grass during the first days, but a worse way through mountains and more dangerous passages than we had experienced previously," Coronado would later write to the viceroy. "The horses were so tired that they were not equal to it, so that in the last desert we lost more horses than before; and some Indian allies and a Spaniard called Spinosa, besides two negroes, died from eating some herbs because the food had given out."

The expedition made slow progress. In the village of Chiametla—less than 200 miles north of the starting-off point of Compostela—a scout met the army. He was exhausted and half-starved. He warned Coronado that he had spent a bitter winter in the despoblado and that many of his Indian servants had died from exposure to the elements. Even worse, the scout said that there might not be any gold ahead. He claimed to have met up with some Indians from Hawikuh, the first of the Seven Cities of Gold. "They have turquoises in quantity, but not so many as the friar said," the scout reported to Coronado.

The scout also told Coronado that danger lurked ahead. He warned that the Zuni Indians were hostile and would attack the expedition.

Still, Coronado and the soldiers trudged on. Food and water ran low, and Coronado was forced to send hunting parties deep into the despoblado to find new supplies. Shortly after the soldiers crossed

These ancient Pueblo Indian ruins are believed to be the site of Hawikuh, the city sought by Coronado in 1540.

what is now the U.S.-Mexican border into the rugged territory of what would become known as Arizona, they arrived at an Indian settlement called

Chichilticalli. Fray Marcos had told them that Chichilticalli was a busy, bustling town of thousands of people. Instead, they found a single, broken-down *hovel* made out of mud.

They pushed on. Finally, on the night of July 6, 1540, they made camp in a valley in Zuni territory in what is now New Mexico. Over the next hill stood Hawikuh—the first of the Seven Cities of Gold. Coronado planned to take a small party the next morning over the hill and seize the riches.

When the Spaniards arose the next morning, they immediately spotted two Indians atop a nearby *mesa*—obviously a scouting party from Hawikuh. The scouts quickly ran away, but more Indians soon assembled on the mesa, shouting at the Spaniards. Coronado's men were startled by the natives, and many saddled their horses backward.

Still, they made their way over the hill and gazed upon Hawikuh.

Instead of a magnificent city of gold, the haggard troop of Spanish soldiers saw only a crowded little village of Indians.

"Such were the curses that some hurled at Fray Marcos, that I pray God may protect him from them," one of the soldiers later wrote.

The Conquistadors

2

In the middle of the eighth century, while Europe was in the Dark Ages, tribes of warriors from North Africa made their way across the Mediterranean Sea and attacked Spain. These warriors were known as the *Moors*, and they would rule Spain from about the year 750 until they were driven out of Spain and neighboring Portugal more than 700 years later.

Although the Moors introduced trade and culture to the area, they were nevertheless regarded as invaders. The Spanish and Portuguese wished to be rid of them. During the time of the Moorish occupation, the people of Spain

This Arab tapestry shows the Christians and Muslim Moors fighting in the city of Mallorca. The Moors were finally forced out of Spain in the year 1492.

told the story of the Seven Bishops. The story was handed down from generation to generation. Of course, it changed each time in the telling until it became a tale of fantastic proportions—a true legend. According to the legend, around the year 1000 the Seven Bishops and their followers escaped the Moors by building boats and sailing west across the

Atlantic Ocean. Eventually, they arrived at a distant land and built seven great cities. They filled the cities with riches. These seven cities would become known as the Seven Cities of Gold.

By the 1500s, after the Moors had returned to North Africa, many people in Spain continued to believe the legend of the Seven Bishops.

* * * *

Francisco Vásquez de Coronado was born in 1510 in Salamanca, a university town in the Spanish *province* of León. He was born to a wealthy family—his father was a nobleman and friend to the king of Spain. Coronado was raised in a large house, attended by servants, and educated in the finest schools. But he was not the oldest of his father's sons. That meant he would not inherit the family wealth, which always went to the eldest son. So Coronado could either live his life in Spain on a small portion of his family's wealth, or he could try to make his fortune on his own.

Coronado decided to leave Spain for the New World across the Atlantic Ocean. Years before, the Spanish armies had defeated the Aztec Indians and colonized Mexico, calling it New Spain. Coronado would have a very influential friend in New Spain:

the viceroy, Antonio de Mendoza. Coronado and Mendoza had known each other in Salamanca. Charles V, the king, had appointed Mendoza viceroy and charged him with overseeing the great land and preserving Spain's interests across the Atlantic. Charles was concerned that many of the Spanish noblemen who had traveled to Mexico were keeping the country's riches for themselves. He wanted a viceroy who would make sure the spoils would remain under the control of the king. Mendoza was fiercely loyal to the king. Coronado also pledged his loyalty to Charles V. Coronado and Mendoza sailed for the New World together.

They arrived in New Spain in 1535 and established homes in Mexico City. Coronado quickly became a man to watch there. His friend the viceroy awarded him a seat on the Mexico City Municipal Council, the body that governed what was becoming a bustling *metropolis*. In 1537, he married Beatriz de Estrada, a daughter in one of the wealthiest families in New Spain.

Coronado soon proved himself an able military commander. When native and black slaves at a nearby silver mine rebelled, Viceroy Mendoza sent Coronado to the mine with a troop of soldiers to put

During the rule of Spain's King Charles, the conquistadors explored large areas of the New World, seeking gold and glory.

down the uprising. Coronado succeeded, and the viceroy was impressed. As a reward, Mendoza made Coronado governor of New Galicia, a province northwest of Mexico City. In fact, four years later, Coronado's search for the Seven Cities would begin in New Galicia's capital, Compostela.

And so Coronado settled into a comfortable life in New Spain. He had wealth through his marriage to Beatriz. He had accomplishments: his victory over the rebellion had made him a respected leader.

He had responsibility: as governor of New Galicia, he served as Mendoza's chief administrator for the province and was responsible for looking out for the king's interests in the region. He was ready to take the next step: to be counted among the ranks of Spain's great explorers.

The country had for years been sending out explorers across the globe to discover new lands and claim their riches for the royal family. In 1492, Queen Isabella of Spain had financed the explorations of Christopher Columbus. An Italian, Columbus intended to explore Asia but instead discovered the islands of the Caribbean. Nevertheless, he planted the Spanish flag in the New World.

In 1519, Hernando Cortés landed in Mexico with an army of 500 soldiers. He defeated a force of thousands of Aztec Indians and claimed Mexico for the king of Spain. Cortés was the first of the great Spanish *conquistadors*, or conquerors. He was not only an explorer, but also a military leader. Other conquistadors followed. By the time Coronado and Mendoza boarded the ship for the New World, the Spanish flag flew from Peru to Mexico.

The conquistadors were after more than just territory to claim in the name of Spain. The conquered lands held great stores of natural resources: precious metals that could be mined; fruits and vegetables that grew in fertile abundance; goods obtained in trade with the Indians; and, of course, the Indians themselves, who would be forced into servitude by the new masters of their land.

What's more, the king of Spain had declared that all Indians in the New World would be converted to Christianity. The Indians were forced to give up their tribal religions and worship God as Christians.

Finally, the Spaniards believed that the New World held great deposits of gold and other treasures, such as silver and jewels. Cortés became the first conquistador to find vast riches when he defeated the Aztecs and found gold, silver, and rare jewels. Later, Francisco Pizarro conquered the Incas and found gold in the mountain palaces of the Inca rulers.

Converting the natives of the New World to Christianity was very important. Catholic Europe believed that at the time of Christ's Second Coming, the whole world should be Christian to meet him. Also, they believed, a person could get into heaven by bringing the "true faith" to new people.

The viceroy of New Spain, Antonio de Mendoza, liked and trusted Francisco Coronado. He asked Coronado to search America to find the Seven Cities of Gold—a mission the conquistador accepted eagerly.

But none of the conquistadors had been able to find the legendary Seven Cities of Gold. Many had tried. In 1528, a Spanish explorer named Pánfilo de Narváez left Cuba with 300 soldiers and was never heard from again. Eight years later, four men turned up in Mexico, claiming to be the only survivors of the Narváez expedition. One of the survivors, Alvar Núñez de Cabeza de Vaca, was brought to Mexico City and given an audience with the new viceroy, Antonio de Mendoza.

Cabeza de Vaca told Mendoza of his eight years of hardship—traveling over seas, through jungles, and across the deserts of the New World.

Had Cabeza de Vaca seen the Seven Cities of Gold? the viceroy asked.

No, Cabeza de Vaca told Mendoza. The lands he had seen were "remote and malign, devoid of resources."

Still, Mendoza pressed Cabeza de Vaca. Mendoza dreamed of outdoing the great Cortés as a treasure finder. He meant to impress the king and, of course, to keep some of the gold for himself.

He asked again: Did Cabeza de Vaca have any knowledge of the Seven Cities?

Perhaps, Cabeza de Vaca said. In the Sonora Valley in Arizona, Cabeza de Vaca had spent time with a tribe of Indians who had spoken of a rich, far-away people with whom they traded. The distant Indians lived in great cities and occupied large houses filled with treasures: **turquoises**, emeralds, and other items. The Indians had told Cabeza de Vaca that the land of the wealthy Indians lay well to the north, beyond the deserts and mountains.

The story enthralled Mendoza, who decided to send a small party to scout the north. If this mission succeeded, Mendoza would organize a full expedition. To lead the small party, he selected Fray Marcos. The scouts left early in 1539, using as a guide a Moroccan-born slave named Estevanico (sometimes called Esteban), one of the four survivors of the Narváez expedition.

It didn't take long for Estevanico and Fray Marcos to start hearing stories of the Seven Cities. A few months after starting out, the scouts encountered an Indian who claimed to have seen the Seven Cities. By May 1539, two Indians sent on ahead by the

At the same time Fray Marcos was searching the Southwest, another expedition was preparing to search for the Seven Cities of Gold. This group, headed by Hernando de Soto, landed in Florida in May 1539.

scouts returned to camp badly wounded. They reported that a local chieftain had imprisoned and tortured them and had executed others in their party. He had sent the survivors back to the camp as a warning for the scouts to stay away. Why was the chieftain so intent on driving off the outsiders? Did he have gold he wished to protect?

The scouts pushed on. Finally, off in the distance, Fray Marcos thought he saw the outline of one of the Seven Cities. He described it as "bigger than the city of Mexico," but decided not to go any closer because he feared he would be killed. So he turned back and returned to Mexico City. Along the way, he claimed to have seen other cities in the distance.

"I was informed that there was much gold, and that the natives trade in vessels and jewels for the ears; and little plates with which they scrape themselves and remove the sweat," Fray Marcos said.

He returned to Mexico City in August, six months after venturing out with the scouting party.

Mendoza heard these stories and decided to mount a full expedition north. The Seven Cities of Gold seemed to be within within his grasp.

To lead the expedition Mendoza turned to his friend, Coronado.

Coronado and his men on the march. When they finally reached Hawikuh, the Spaniards were disappointed to find it was just a small village—not a city of gold.

The Battle of Hawikuh 3

espite all the warnings along the way that Fray Marcos hadn't told the truth about what he knew of the Seven Cities, Coronado and his men were still surprised when they fixed their eyes on Hawikuh. Instead of a vast, rich, city teeming with thousands of wealthy Indians, the Spaniards saw merely a village carved into the rugged landscape of New Mexico. Yes, the village was walled—but not with great stones as they had imagined. Hawikuh was a *pueblo*: a village of huts and houses surrounded by a wall made of *adobe*—sun-dried clay that could be fashioned into bricks. Later, the Spaniards would estimate the population of Hawikuh at 800.

"It was a little crowded village, looking as if it had been crumpled all up together," wrote Pedro de Castaneda. "There are **haciendas** in New Spain which make a better appearance at a distance."

The Zuni Indians who occupied the pueblo were not friendly. A band of armed Zunis approached Coronado's men. Coronado, through his Indian interpreters, tried to communicate with the Zunis. He wanted them to surrender and swear their allegiance to the king of Spain. He also told them he had arrived to "protect" them, meaning that he wished them to become Christians. He was, after all, following the order of King Charles V to convert all Indians in the New World to Christianity.

The Zunis would not submit. They fired arrows at the Spaniards, who found themselves ducking for cover. The Battle of Hawikuh was on.

The Spaniards regrouped. Shouting their battle cry, "Santiago!" (the Spanish word for St. James, the soldier-saint of Spain), the men rushed the walled village. By the time they got to the walls, they had killed about a dozen Zunis.

The remaining Zunis outside the pueblo retreated up ladders along the walls. These ladders

Hawikuh must have looked much like this pueblo when
Coronado and his men stumbled upon the Zuni village.
Although Coronado was wounded during the attack on
the pueblo, the Indians were no match for the Spaniards.

enabled the residents of Hawikuh to enter and leave
the village. When Coronado and his men made it to
the bottom of the ladders, they found themselves
pelted with rocks and arrows from the Indians sta-
tioned atop the walls.

Coronado was a marked man. His gilded armor shone in the bright sunshine, making him a special target. As he scaled a ladder he was struck by a rock and knocked to the ground below. Coronado got to his feet. Then he was hit again.

"They knocked me down to the ground twice with countless great stones which they threw down from above, and if I had not been protected by the very good headpiece which I wore, I think that the outcome would have been bad for me," Coronado wrote to Viceroy Mendoza. "My men picked me up from the ground, however, with two small wounds in my face and an arrow in my foot, and with many bruises on my arms and legs, and in this condition I retired from the battle, very weak. I think that if Don García López de Cárdenas had not come to my help, like a good cavalier, the second time that they knocked me to the ground, by placing his own body above mine, I should have been in much greater danger than I was."

Coronado was carried away from the battle. Meanwhile, his men pressed the attack. Although the Indians had the protection of the wall, their weapons could not match those carried by the Spaniards. The Indians were armed with spears and bows; the Spaniards carried the guns called arque-buses. The Indians had never seen firearms before, and they had no defense against them. Slowly, the Spaniards made their way up the ladders, driving the Zuni defenders off the walls. The soldiers were in the village now, and they marched through the narrow alleys of Hawikuh, rounding up Zunis and killing those who tried to fight back. The pueblo was now in the hands of Coronado's men. The Battle of Hawikuh had taken less than an hour.

Coronado ordered the rest of the army to join him. He also sent small raiding parties to nearby Zuni villages. There were a total of seven villages in the region the Spaniards would call Cíbola. But none of them resembled a City of Gold in any way. The raiding parties had little trouble defeating the Zuni defenders; each village fell as quickly as Hawikuh.

What became of Fray Marcos, the friar whose tales of wealthy Indian cities prompted Viceroy Mendoza to mount the expedition? Coronado had brought the friar along to act as a guide to the Seven Cities. Now Coronado was eager to rid himself of Fray Marcos. The friar was sent back to Mexico City. Coronado would soon speak of the friar in harsh words.

"I can assure you," Coronado wrote to Viceroy Mendoza, "that in reality he has not told you the truth in a single thing. The Seven Cities are seven little villages, all within a radius of five leagues." (A league is a unit of measurement, roughly equal to three miles.)

Although the men found no gold in Hawikuh and the other six villages, they did find good food. They ate the Zunis' corn, squash, and chickens. For an army that had endured a rugged trail with little to eat, food must have been as valued as any piece of gold or fancy jewel.

They learned more about their new hosts. The Zunis were farmers and maintained agricultural lands surrounding their pueblo. The farms included simple irrigation systems that brought water to the crops. The corn they grew was known as *maize*–not the yellow, sweet corn we eat today, but a hard kernel, colorful corn that could withstand the hot sun and arid desert air. The maize was ground up to make flat cakes that came to be known by the Spaniards as tortillas.

"They make the best corn cakes I have seen anywhere and that is what everybody ordinarily eats. They have the very best arrangement and method

The natives of the Southwest used turquoise to make attractive jewelry. However, this did not interest the conquistadors, who were seeking gold. In the background of this photo is an adobe church, probably built by Spanish missionaries.

for grinding corn that was ever seen. One of these Indian women here will grind as much flour as four of the Mexicans do," wrote Coronado.

Despite the hostile reception Coronado got from the Zunis when he approached their village, he soon learned that the Indians were for the most part a peace-loving people. Indeed, Coronado and his men grew to admire the Zunis.

The Zunis were skilled in pottery making and other crafts. They fashioned decorative jars and bowls out of clay and adorned them with images of their gods. Weavers crafted straw baskets that were amazingly tight and able to hold water.

Good food and fine pottery were certainly treasures to be valued, but gold was still very much on the minds of the Spaniards. Granted, there were no Seven Cities of Gold in Cíbola, but that didn't mean the Seven Cities didn't exist. The country was vast and unexplored. Who knew what one could find over the next mountain or across the next desert?

The Zunis provided an answer. Eager to be rid of the Spaniards, they told their conquerors that riches could be found to the northwest. Coronado was eager to investigate the story. He needed to rest to recover from his injuries, so he couldn't personally lead the expedition. Instead, he sent a party of 20 soldiers to explore.

The men marched for 75 miles, encountering many Indian villages along the way. These were the villages of the Hopi Indians. None of them resembled a City of Gold. Finally, the disappointed band of soldiers returned to Cíbola and reported to Coronado that they found no gold, although they did tell the leader about a great river they had heard about west of the Hopi lands.

Coronado was intrigued. Still too weak to investigate himself, he dispatched another small band of soldiers to find the river. He placed the party under the leadership of a **lieutenant** named García López de Cárdenas, the man who had shielded the fallen Coronado during the Battle of Hawikuh. Cárdenas followed the trail of the previous expedition into Arizona. He quickly found the Hopi villages. Accompanied by some Hopis who agreed to serve as guides, the Cárdenas party made its way through a stark desert and over rugged mountains.

The journey took 20 days and was not easy. Pedro de Castaneda, who didn't make the trip but received a description of the journey from members of the party, would later write, "This region was high and covered with low and twisting pine trees; it was extremely cold, being open to the north."

Suddenly, the party stopped in its tracks. Before them was a huge opening in the earth, 10 to 15 miles wide. Below, the walls dipped straight down over sheer rock. And far below, more than a mile down, they saw a river snaking its way through the gorge.

Cárdenas and the others were the first European explorers to gaze upon the Grand Canyon and, down below, the Colorado River.

Great Discoveries 4

erhaps it was the discovery of the majestic Grand Canyon, or perhaps it was the realization, finally, that the Seven Cities did not exist, but Coronado found himself changing. No longer did he regard himself as a conquistador who would return in triumph with the riches of a vanquished people. Instead, Coronado now saw himself as an explorer. He was far more interested in traveling throughout the vast and great land north of Mexico, chronicling what he found and searching for new wonders.

"I have determined to send men throughout all the surrounding regions in order to find out whether there is anything, and to suffer any extremity rather than give up this enterprise," Coronado wrote to Viceroy Mendoza.

The Grand Canyon and Colorado River would be only the first of the discoveries Coronado and his lieutenants would record as they made their way over six future states of the United States: Arizona, New Mexico, California, Oklahoma, Kansas, and Texas. Their trek would carry them over 6,000 miles of American territory and through villages that would eventually become important American cities—Albuquerque and Taos in New Mexico and Great Bend in Kansas, among others.

As for Cárdenas, the lieutenant and his men found they could gaze at the Grand Canyon and the Colorado River below, but they could go little further. For three days, Cárdenas and his men searched for a trail down into the massive canyon. Indeed, they were in desperate need of water. Although the mighty Colorado River rushed by them, just a mile or so below, they had no way to reach it.

"The three lightest and most agile men went down until those who were above were unable to keep sight of them," wrote Castaneda. "They returned about 4 o'clock in the afternoon. They said they had been down about a third of the way and that the river seemed very large."

So Cárdenas and his men were forced to turn back and head for Cíbola to report their findings to Coronado. Cárdenas failed to find a trail down to the river. Others who came

> The Grand Canyon was formed over a period of about a million years. Its gorge was created by the rushing Colorado River. The river cut through the terrain and, through erosion, created the wide canyon.

after him would fail, too. In 1850, an expedition mounted by the U.S. Army would finally find a trail down to the Colorado River from above.

Meanwhile, Coronado had dispatched a second group of explorers. This one was headed by a lieutenant named Pedro de Tovar. The Tovar expedition headed northwest in search of a region the Spaniards called Tusayan. They had been told there were seven villages in Tusayan. Could these be the Seven Cities of Gold? The rumor was worth tracking down.

Tovar's men soon came to a sprawling desert like no others they had seen in their travels. The soils of this desert were purple, gray, and dark red. In the

A typical scene of native life in an Southwestern Indian village. Coronado and his men saw many sights like this on their journeys through the Plains.

morning, the desert seemed to turn blue. At night it was a blazing red. The region would come to be known as the Painted Desert.

Tovar eventually found Tusayan. But he soon came to realize it was not an area of riches. It was simply an Indian pueblo.

Coronado dispatched a third scout party led by a lieutenant named Melchior Díaz. Díaz was ordered to head west with the hope that he would eventually find the Pacific coast. There, he could meet up with supply ships that had been dispatched by Viceroy Mendoza to replenish the expedition's dwindling stores of food and gunpowder, as well as provide horses and other essentials.

Díaz and 25 Spanish soldiers, as well as some Indian guides, made their way over a vast desert, crossing back over the border into Mexico. After trudging for 300 miles, the Díaz party came across the Colorado River—the same river Cárdenas and his men had found far to the north. The people of this area were the Yuma Indians—tall, athletic people who exhibited incredible strength. Díaz decided to capture one of the Yumas to show Viceroy Mendoza. Four Spaniards cornered a young Yuma and attempted to make him their prisoner, but the Yuma fought them off.

The men returned to the trail, pushing on with their mission to find the supply ships. They followed the Colorado River until they cut back across the Mexican border and entered what would become California. There, they came across a large tree with a message carved into its trunk. The message, written in Spanish, instructed the men to dig up some letters that had been buried beneath the tree. They found the letters and learned that the captain of the supply ships had sailed up the Colorado River and had waited a long time for the soldiers. But he had been forced to leave because the ships had started breaking apart.

Although the mission to meet the supply ships failed, the Díaz party would become the first explorers to enter California by an overland route.

Castaneda wrote about what Díaz and the soldiers found in California: "They came upon some beds of burning lava. No one could cross them, for it would be like going into the sea to drown. It was amazing to see the cinders boil, for it looked like something infernal. They turned away from this place because it seemed so dangerous."

What had they found? Díaz and his men had entered California's Imperial Valley, where they had discovered the state's famous hot springs.

As for Díaz, he would not return to Cíbola to report his findings to Coronado. He suffered an accident on the expedition, falling off his horse. He died a few days later.

Back at Cíbola, there were other discoveries to be made. Coronado had been visited by a group of Indians from Cicuye, a pueblo 200 miles to the east beyond a land known as Tiguex. Messages about Coronado's expedition, and the Spaniards' terrible weapons, had reached the Indians. They cautiously approached the explorer to assure him he could travel through their land in peace. They also invited Coronado to visit their homes.

Coronado dispatched Captain Hernando de Alvarado to accompany the Indians back to Cicuye. Alvarado, who made the trek with 20 soldiers, reached Tiguex after about a week of riding, where he found pueblos lining both shores of the river that today we know as the Upper Rio Grande. He found the Indians of the pueblos friendly. He sent word back to Coronado inviting the commander to join him. Five days later, Alvarado reached Cicuye, a large pueblo. A soldier who rode with Alvarado would later write: "Its houses are four and five stories high, some of them being very fine. These people neither plant cotton nor raise turkeys because it is close to the plains where the cattle roam."

The cattle the soldier wrote about were really buffalo. Although the Spaniards had seen Indians

When Hernando de Alvarado was exploring the Southwest, millions of buffalo roamed the plains. This painting by Karl Bodmer shows two Indians, wearing coyote skins, creeping up on the herd.

wearing buffalo skins, they had never seen the burly, majestic, humpbacked animals for themselves. Alvarado and his men were the first Europeans to see American bison.

"The most monstrous beasts ever seen or read about" is how one soldier described them.

It is estimated that in Coronado's day—well before the American bison was virtually wiped out by buffalo hunters—more than 60 million buffalo lived on the Great Plains.

By now, Coronado had fully recovered from the injuries he suffered during the Battle of Hawikuh. He had decided to follow Alvarado to Tiguex, where he spent the winter of 1540–41. He found trouble there. When he arrived, he discovered that Alvarado had taken as hostages the two head chiefs from Cicuye. Cárdenas, who had made his way back from the Grand Canyon, had also infuriated the Indians of Tiguex when he kicked them out of their pueblos so that his soldiers could spend the winter in the comfortable homes rather than in tents. Coronado fanned the flames himself when he ordered the Indians of Tiguex to supply him with cotton for his men's bedding. When the Indians refused, Coronado had his men seize the cotton.

All these events led to some *skirmishes* between the Indians and the Spaniards. Then, one morning, some Indians raided a Spanish corral, driving away about 30 horses. The soldiers responded by setting a pueblo on fire. Hundreds of Indians died. Next, Coronado's men attacked Moho, an Indian village. They surrounded the pueblo and tried to take it by force, but they were repelled. Instead, the soldiers settled in for a long *siege*.

By March 1541, the chiefs of Moho asked for a meeting with Coronado. They asked the Spanish leader for permission to let their women and children out of the pueblo. Coronado agreed, allowing them to pass through his ranks. Two weeks later the men in the pueblo attempted an escape, trying to slip through the Spanish ranks under cover of darkness. They were unsuccessful and were all caught or killed by the soldiers. The siege of Moho was over.

By April, Coronado had decided to leave Tiguex. Clearly, the natives did not want the Spaniards to stay, and there were, after all, new lands to explore. He decided to head east in search of Quivira, a city of supposed vast riches.

Apparently, Coronado's discoveries of the great natural wonders of America had not totally quenched his thirst for the conquistador's gold. He had been told of Quivira by an Indian captive whom the Spaniards had named El Turco because his dark complexion reminded them of a Turk.

The Indian captive El Turco guides Coronado and his men as they search for the city of Quivira. Lured by rumors of great treasure, the Spaniards searched for Quivira during the spring and summer of 1541.

Coronado soon arrived in what would one day be called Texas. The terrain was rugged and stark. The weather was hot and dry. Steep cliffs made travel difficult. Years later, this area of northern Texas would be known as the Panhandle.

As for Quivira, Coronado decided to lead a party of about 30 soldiers north in search of the elusive city of riches. It took Coronado more than a month to march his men out of the rough Panhandle landscape, but at last they reached grassy plains. This area would one day be called Oklahoma.

The men pushed on. They reached the Arkansas River. They were in Kansas now. Had they reached Quivira, a city of riches? Hardly. The villages they found along the Arkansas River were composed mostly of grass huts. It was clear that the Indians who lived in these huts were poor people, able to raise just enough food to maintain their lives. Still, Francisco Coronado was impressed by the beauty of the rolling grasslands.

"The country itself is the best I have ever seen for producing all the products of Spain, for besides the land being very flat and black, and being well watered by the rivulets and springs and rivers, I found

Coronado did not realize it, but his party was only about 300 miles away from another group of Spaniards exploring the New World. This group, under Hernando de Soto, was also unable to find gold as it wandered through Florida and Arkansas. De Soto is credited with discovering the Mississippi River, but he did not survive the expedition.

prunes and nuts and very good sweet grapes and mulberries," Coronado would later write.

And yet, he had once again failed to find gold. By August, Coronado had given up. The treasure of Quivira was no more a reality than the Seven Cities of Gold had been.

True, there were many natural wonders in the thousands of square miles Coronado and his men had explored: vast canyons, rushing rivers, rugged terrain, grassy plains, colorful deserts. But there was no gold.

The Spaniards headed for home.

Coronado's Treasure

5

For Coronado and his soldiers, all there was to do now was to return to Mexico City. The journey home was long, tiring, uneventful, and sad. From the grassy plains of Kansas, they made their way back to Tiguex, where they spent the winter of 1541–42. That winter, Coronado was thrown from his horse and kicked in the head by the animal. He was severely injured and required months to recover. Finally, in the spring of 1542, the men trudged south and crossed the border into New Spain. They arrived in Mexico City in the summer. It had been about two and a half years since they had set out from Compostela.

"The despoblado was traversed without incident," wrote Pedro de Castaneda.

Along the way, the men stopped and erected a huge wooden cross. At the foot of the cross they cut an inscription. It read: "Francisco Vásquez de Coronado, general of the army, had reached this place."

It was a far different army from the one that the people of Compostela had turned out to cheer on its way north. Fewer than 100 of the 300 original Spanish soldiers accompanied Coronado into Mexico City. The others had either died through injury or disease during the expedition or had deserted out of fear that their deeds against the helpless Indians would land them in trouble with the authorities in Mexico City. Hundreds of the Indian servants didn't make it back either. And several friars who had accompanied Coronado stayed behind in the pueblos to teach Christianity to the Indians. They soon lost their lives as well. Without the soldiers to protect them, they fell victim to the Indians, who had little taste for the religion of the Europeans.

The Indians who had met the Spaniards along the way fared little better. Many died in the bloody battles Coronado and his men waged against them. Others became slaves or servants. And many died

where God Our Lord might be served," Coronado wrote to the king. He went on to say, "There were none of the things there of which Fray Marcos had told. There is not any gold nor any other metal—nothing but little villages."

No gold.

But there was treasure, although in a far different form than the one Coronado had imagined.

Coronado had explored a vast land and beheld wonders no other European had experienced: the Painted Desert, the Texas Panhandle, the Grand Canyon, the Colorado River, the plains of Oklahoma and Kansas. His men had seen buffalo grazing in large numbers on the prairies. In years to come, these great natural wonders would become valued resources of a mighty nation. Of course, Coronado had no way of knowing all that in 1542.

And Coronado would also have no way of knowing that he had brought a culture to the region that would live on into the 21st century. Indeed, he was the first Spanish explorer to visit what would become the American Southwest. Others would follow. In the 1590s, General Juan de Oñate established a settlement in what would become known as Taos, New Mexico. In 1610, Pedro de Peralto

Francisco Coronado brought Spanish religion and culture to the natives of the American Southwest. This native painting on cloth shows Indians being baptized.

brought a group of settlers to a new settlement in New Mexico he named Santa Fe, or "Holy Faith." Today Santa Fe is the capital city of New Mexico. Elsewhere, great cities throughout the Southwest carry Spanish names: Los Angeles in California, Las Vegas in Nevada, San Antonio in Texas. The art, architecture, and customs of many of these cities are flavored with a definite Spanish influence. No other region of America is so dominated by the culture of a single people.

After his return, Coronado found himself out of favor with Viceroy Mendoza. His friend never again gave Coronado an important mission. Coronado had spent his wife's fortune on the expedition. Now, back in New Spain, he was penniless. What's more, he was brought to trial on charges of mishandling the expedition and committing crimes against the Indians. He eventually was found not guilty, but Mendoza was forced to remove his friend from the post of governor of New Galicia. Coronado died in obscurity at the age of 44.

But he would not be forgotten. Coronado would eventually be honored by the country he helped open up to new exploration. Today, you can find Coronado National Park near Tucson in southeast Arizona. The land is largely untouched, and visitors can see the same rocky terrain and stark desert that Coronado and his men found centuries ago. Many of the original trails in the park have been preserved. Indeed, visitors to the park can travel over some of the same trails taken by Coronado's soldiers nearly 500 years ago.

Chronology

1510 Francisco Vásquez de Coronado is born in Salamanca, Spain.

1521 Hernando Cortés becomes the first of the great Spanish conquistadors when he defeats the Aztecs in Mexico and seizes their treasures.

1535 Coronado and Antonio de Mendoza, the new viceroy of New Spain, arrive in Mexico City.

1536 Four men emerge from the *despoblado* and claim to be the survivors of the ill-fated expedition of Pánfilo de Narváez. Mendoza is convinced they have knowledge of the Seven Cities of Gold.

1538 Coronado becomes governor of New Galicia, Mexico.

1539 Mendoza sends Fray Marcos de Niza on a scouting party north; Marcos returns, claiming to know the location of the Seven Cities.

1540 Mendoza selects Coronado to lead the expedition in search of the Seven Cities. He leaves in February and quickly finds Hawikuh, the first city, but discovers that the city is no more than an Indian pueblo. Other searches for gold also prove futile, but Coronado's lieutenants find the Grand Canyon and Colorado River, the Painted Desert, herds of buffalo, and other natural wonders of America.

1541 Coronado travels through the Texas Panhandle as well as the plains of Oklahoma and Kansas.

1542 Coronado returns to New Spain, penniless and with no gold to show for his 6,000-mile journey.

1545 Coronado is tried and found not guilty on charges of mishandling the expedition and committing crimes against the Indians.

1554 Coronado dies in Mexico City on September 22.

Glossary

adobe—bricks made of mud and dried in the sun.

arquebus—a heavy firearm carried by Spanish soldiers in the 16th century.

allegiance—loyalty owed by a subject to a ruler, or by a citizen to a government.

cavalry—soldiers who fight while mounted on horses.

conquistadors—Spanish soldiers who conquered native peoples in the New World.

expedition—a journey made by a group of people for a specific purpose, such as exploration or conquest.

despoblado—a Spanish word meaning "uninhabited area" or "desolate wilderness."

ducat—a coin, usually made of gold, that was used in various European countries and colonies.

fray (pronounced "fry")—a Spanish friar or religious brother.

gilded—coated with gold.

hacienda—a large estate or plantation in Mexico; also the main house on such a plantation.

hovel—a small, poorly made house or hut.

immunity—a natural protection from disease. The natives of the New World were not immune to diseases carried by European explorers, so they were at greater risk of dying from the diseases.

lieutenant—an assistant commander.

maize—Indian corn.

mesa—a flat-topped hill or mountain surrounded by lower

ground.

metropolis–a large, important city.

Moors–Arabs from North Africa who invaded Spain in the
eighth century. Because the Moors followed Islam, they
were involved in a series of bloody wars with the Christian people of Spain and the rest of Europe. The Moors
were forced out of Spain in 1492.

province–a region of a country, usually separated from other
provinces for geographical or political reasons.

pueblo–an Indian village in the American Southwest.

siege–a military tactic whereby a city or town is surrounded,
thus cutting off its supplies and pressuring its defenders
to surrender.

skirmish–a brief or minor fight in a larger conflict.

turquoise–a blue or greenish-blue gemstone.

viceroy–the governor of a colony or province who rules as the
representative of a king or queen.

Further Reading

Cabeza de Vaca, Alvar Núñez. *The Account: Alvar Núñez Cabeza de Vaca's Relación.* Houston: Arte Publico, 1993.

Castaneda, Pedro de. *The Journey of Coronado.* Mineola, NY: Dover Publications, 1990.

Jacobs, William J. *Coronado: Dreamer in Golden Armor.* Danbury, CT: Franklin Watts, 1994.

Lavender, David S. *De Soto, Coronado, Cabrillo: Explorers of the Northern Mystery.* Washington, D.C.: National Park Service Division of Publications, 1992.

Preston, Douglas J. *Cities of Gold: A Journey Across the American Southwest.* Santa Fe: Museum of New Mexico Press, 1999.

———. "Following—Painfully—the Route of Coronado After 450 Years." *Smithsonian 57* (January 1990).

Stein, R. Conrad. *The World's Great Explorers: Francisco de Coronado.* Chicago: Children's Press Inc., 1992.

Time-Life books. *The Spanish West.* New York: Time-Life, 1976.

Udall, Stewart C., and Jerry D. Jacka. *Majestic Journey: Coronado's Inland Empire.* Santa Fe: Museum of New Mexico Press, 1995

Picture Credits

HAL MARCOVITZ is a journalist for the *Allentown Morning Call* in Pennsylvania. In 1993 and 1996, his columns were awarded the Keystone Press Award by the Pennsylvania Newspaper Publishers Association. His first book was the satirical novel *Painting the White House*. He has also written a biography of Marco Polo for Chelsea House's EXPLORERS OF NEW WORLDS series. He lives in Chalfont, Pennsylvania, with his wife, Gail, and daughters Michelle and Ashley.